Giant Weta

The World's Biggest Grasshopper

by Natalie Lunis

Consultant: Peter Smithers, Entomologist
School of Biomedical and Biological Sciences
University of Plymouth, England

New York, New York

Credits

Cover, TOC, © Ingrid Visser/Minden Pictures/FLPA; 4–5, © Thierry Berrod/Mona Lisa Production/Science Photo Library; 6, © www.rodmorris.co.nz; 8, © Alan Greensmith/ardea.com; 9, © www.rodmorris.co.nz; 10, © Julian W/Shutterstock; 11, 12, 13, 14, 15, 16, 17, 18, 19, 20, © www.rodmorris.co.nz; 21, © Ingrid Visser/Minden Pictures/FLPA; 22L, © Bruce Davidson/naturepl.com; 22C, © Nick Gordon/ardea.com; 22R, 23TL, © Andrew Burgess/Shutterstock; 23TR, © www.rodmorris.co.nz; 23BL, © Jitka Volfova/Shutterstock; 23BR, © Kiwi Mikex.

Publisher: Kenn Goin
Senior Editor: Joyce Tavolacci
Creative Director: Spencer Brinker
Photo Researcher: Calcium Creative

Library of Congress Cataloging-in-Publication Data

Lunis, Natalie.
  Giant weta : the world's biggest grasshopper / by Natalie Lunis.
     pages ; cm. -- (Even more supersized!)
  Audience: 6-9.
  Includes bibliographical references and index.
  ISBN 978-1-61772-731-3 (library binding) -- ISBN 1-61772-731-8 (library binding)
  1. Giant wetas--Juvenile literature. 2. Grasshoppers--Juvenile literature. I. Title.

  QL508.A56L86 2013
  595.7'26--dc23

                          2012033777

For more information, write to Bearport Publishing Company, Inc., 45 West 21st Street, Suite 3B, New York, New York 10010. Printed in the United States of America.

10 9 8 7 6 5 4 3 2 1

Contents

A Giant Grasshopper

The giant weta (WAYT-uh) is the world's biggest grasshopper.

This **insect** can weigh up to 2.5 ounces (71 g), or as much as three mice.

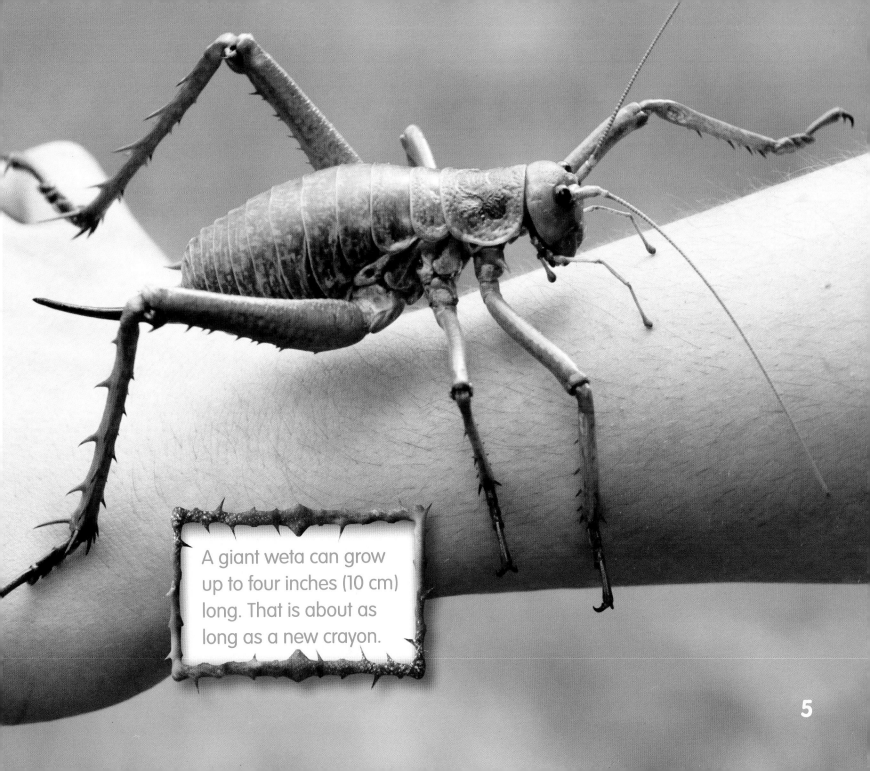

A giant weta can grow up to four inches (10 cm) long. That is about as long as a new crayon.

Island Homes

There are 11 kinds of giant wetas.

These big grasshoppers live on a few islands that are part of New Zealand.

The largest weta of all is the Little Barrier Island giant weta.

It is named for the small island on which it is found.

New Zealand is a country in the Pacific Ocean. It is made up of two large islands and many smaller islands.

Little Barrier Island
Giant Wetas in the Wild

Australia

Little Barrier
Island

New Zealand

Pacific Ocean

 Where Little Barrier
Island giant wetas live

Rat Attack

Giant wetas once lived all over New Zealand.

Then, hundreds of years ago, people from other parts of the world moved to New Zealand.

The boats they traveled on often had rats living in them.

Over time, the rats left the boats and spread all over the islands.

In many places, they hunted and ate most of the giant wetas.

Pacific rat

The kind of rat that hunts the Little Barrier Island weta is called the Pacific rat, or kiore.

giant weta

Hiding Out

Rats are not the only enemy of giant wetas.

Birds, lizards, and bats hunt them too.

To stay safe from these animals, giant wetas spend most of the day hiding.

Some hide in tree bark or on branches.

Others hide under rocks or in holes in the ground.

tuatara

The tuatara also hunts giant wetas. It is a medium-sized reptile that lives in parts of New Zealand.

baby weta

tree bark

giant weta hiding

Nighttime Meals

Giant wetas come out at night to eat.

Leaves and fruit are their main foods.

Using their strong jaws, wetas tear and chew plant parts.

Sometimes, giant wetas eat insects that they find in the forest.

jaws

moss

Moving Around

Like all grasshoppers, giant wetas have six legs.

Most grasshoppers use their large back legs to jump.

However, the New Zealand giants are too heavy to jump.

Instead, they walk or crawl to move from place to place.

Sometimes, giant wetas use **spikes** on their long back legs to defend themselves. They lift their legs into the air to frighten or scratch an attacker.

spike

Hatching from Eggs

Giant wetas begin their lives growing in tiny eggs.

An adult female lays up to 300 eggs in the dirt.

The babies that come out of the eggs look like their mother, but they are much smaller.

baby weta

adult weta

newly hatched wetas

When baby wetas hatch, they are about one half inch (1.3 cm) long.

eggs

Getting Bigger

Giant wetas, like all insects, have a hard covering called an **exoskeleton**.

As a weta grows, its exoskeleton becomes too small and tight.

The insect forms a new, bigger exoskeleton and wriggles out of its old one.

This set of changes is called **molting**.

It takes about 18 months for a giant weta to grow to adult size. During this time, it can molt up to nine times.

weta molting

old
exoskeleton

new
exoskeleton

More to Learn

Scientists study giant wetas in the wild to learn more about them.

As they do, scientists sometimes discover new kinds of grasshoppers.

Perhaps one day they will find one that is even bigger than the giant weta!

In parts of New Zealand, scientists attach tiny radios to the bodies of giant wetas to learn more about where they go and how they survive.

radio transmitter

More Big Insects

Giant wetas belong to a group of animals called insects. All insects have six legs and a body that has three main parts. Most insects hatch from eggs. While almost all insects have wings, some do not.

Here are three more big insects.

Goliath Beetle

The goliath beetle is a big, bulky beetle. It weighs about 1.8 ounces (51 g) and grows up to 4.3 inches (11 cm) long.

Titan Beetle

The titan beetle is the world's biggest beetle. It weighs 1.2 ounces (34 g) and can grow to be 6.6 inches (16.8 cm) long.

Giant Burrowing Cockroach

The giant burrowing cockroach is the largest cockroach in the world. It weighs around 1.1 ounces (31.2 g) and can grow to be three inches (7.6 cm) long.

Giant Weta
2.5 ounces/71 g

Goliath Beetle
1.8 ounces/51 g

Titan Beetle
1.2 ounces/34 g

Giant Burrowing Cockroach
1.1 ounces/31.2 g

Glossary

exoskeleton
(*eks*-oh-SKEL-uh-tuhn)
the hard covering
that protects an
insect's body

molting
(MOHLT-ing) when
an insect sheds
its exoskeleton

insect (IN-sekt)
a small animal that
has six legs, three
main body parts,
two antennas,
and a hard
covering called
an exoskeleton

spikes (SPIKES)
hard, sharp points

23

Index

Read More

Goldish, Meish. *Leaping Grasshoppers (No Backbone! The World of Invertebrates)*. New York: Bearport (2008).

Markle, Sandra. *Insects (Biggest! Littlest!)*. Honesdale, PA: Boyds Mills Press (2009).

Packard, Mary. *Goliath Beetle: One of the World's Heaviest Insects (SuperSized!)*. New York: Bearport (2007).

Learn More Online

To learn more about giant wetas, visit
bearportpublishing.com/EvenMoreSuperSized